ur

d-

d

er

Guildhall, just a stone's throw from King Alfred's Statue at the bottom end of the High Street.

Tel: 01962 840 500

Email: tourism@winchester.gov.uk

Web: www.visitwinchester.co.uk

To find out more about **Winchester Cathedra**l please go to:

www.winchester-cathedral.org.uk

WINCHESTER

A Little Souvenir

CHRIS ANDREWS PUBLICATIONS LTD

9/24
£2

The City from St Catharine's Hill

WINCHESTER

Introduction

Winchester is a delightful unspoilt Cathedral city in southern England, situated on The South Downs and with the River Itchen running through it, the city was the former seat of King Alfred the Great and remained the capital of Wessex, and then England, until some time after the Norman Conquest when the capital was moved to London.

The city has many historic buildings, but is particularly known for its Cathedral, originally built in 1079. It has the longest medieval nave in Europe and contains much fine architecture from the 11th to the 16th century. The Cathedral is the place of interment of numerous Bishops of Winchester (such as William of Wykeham), Anglo-Saxon monarchs (Egbert of Wessex) and later monarchs such as King Canute and William Rufus, as well as the authors Jane Austen and Izaak Walton. It was once an important pilgrimage centre and housed the shrine of Saint Swithun.

The Cathedral was built on the site of an older church, a plan of which can be seen to the north of the present construction and is part Norman, extended around the 1200's and the nave remodelled in the Perpendicular style around 1400. The building was saved from serious damage in the early 1900's by a team including a deep sea diver, William Walker who worked

The Cathedral

6 Abbey House, the official residence of the Mayor of Winchester

for some 5 years in the murky wet of the marshy ground under the foundations, underpinning the structure to prevent collapse. The Cathedral has fine chantrys and chapels as well as a library containg rare and valuable books. The stained glass is from several periods and compliments the many tombs, screens, statues and memorials which may be seen inside.

Winchester boasts many other historical monuments and fine houses including Wolvesey Castle, a ruin of the Norman bishop's palace dating from 1110. Abbey House is a fine 18th century town house built on the site of a former monastery, now the mayor's official residence and a house in College Street was lived in by the author Jane Austen for the last six weeks of her life.

Winchester College, a public school founded by William of Wykeham, still largely dates from the first buildings begun in 1382. There are two courtyards, a gatehouse, cloister, hall, a magnificent college chapel and it also owns "The Water Meadows" which have a part of the River Itchen through it. It was planned to educate poor boys before they moved on to New College, Oxford and a life in the church.

Winchester College

Winchester is also known for the Great Hall of its castle, which was built in the 12th century. The Great Hall was rebuilt, sometime between 1222-1235, and still exists in this form. It is famous for King Arthur's Round Table, which has hung in the hall from at least 1463. The table actually dates from the 13th century, and as such is not contemporary to Arthur, despite this it is still of considerable historical interest. The table was originally unpainted, but was painted for King Henry VIII in 1520. The names of the legendary Knights of the Round Table are written around the edge of the table surmounted by King Arthur on his throne. Opposite the table are Prince Charles' 'Wedding Gates'.
In the grounds of the Great Hall is a

 The Great Hall with the Prince Charles Wedding Gates

recreation of a medieval garden. Apart from the hall, only a few excavated remains of the stronghold survive amongst the modern Law Courts.

Outside the city there are country walks in fine chalk downs, with dramatic hills and extensive woodlands, including about a mile to the south the Hospital of St Cross whose almshouses and vast Norman chapel were founded by Henry de Blois in the 1130s. Since at least the 14th century, and still available today, a 'wayfarer's dole' of ale and bread has been handed out there. It was supposedly instigated to aid pilgrims on their route through to Canterbury.

Winchester is a compact collection of interesting buildings and sites, many of them free to enter. It is surrounded by classic English countryside with rewarding views. The images in this litle book hope to give an indication of the variety and charm to be found.

12 Statue of King Alfred in the Broadway, by Thornycroft

14 A detail from one of Winchester's many bookshops

The Guildhall

16 The River Itchen

Weirs Walk

18 The City Mill

View from Abbey Gardens

20 Busy city centre cafe and shops

Inside the Wykeham Arms

22 Priory Gate leading to Cheyney Court and the Cathedral

Cheyney Court

Roman Mosaic now located in the Deanery Porch

26 Bookshop outside the Deanery of Winchester Cathedral

Arcading on the outside of Winchester Cathedral Nave

28 The Cathedral Tower

The Cathedral North Transept

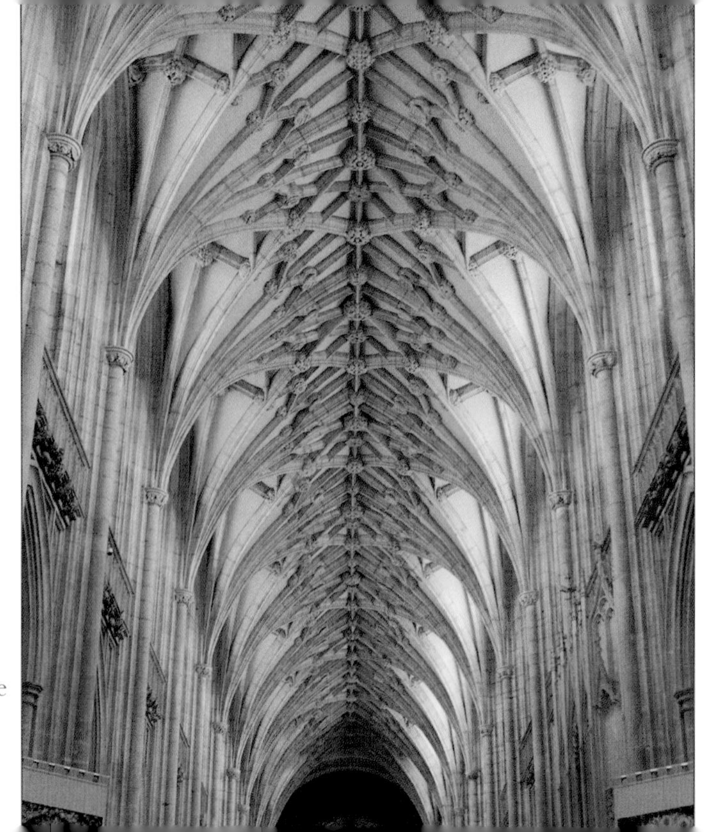

Aisle on the south of the Nave and the Crypt with the statue *Sound II* by Antony Gormley

32 Stained glass in the Cathedral

Effigy of Bishop Waynflete (1447–86), Chancellor of England, headmaster of Winchester College, provost of Eton and founder of Magdalen College, Oxford.

34 The High Altar and William Walker's diving apparatus

The 12th century marble font, with carvings depicting the legends of St Nicholas

36 The Nave with Batik banners

Decorations on the City Museum

38 Winchester Cathedral and city centre from St Giles' Hill

The city from the south

Winchester from the east

42 Winchester College, New Field and school buildings

Winchester College Cloister

Pupils at the College entering Hall

'The Trusty Servant', a College icon

"Illumina", an annual College celebration, formerly book burning, now (usually) less literature and more wood and candles...

46 Wolvesey Palace ruins

The Bishop's Chapel and residence through the ruins

48 Local lunch, smoked trout and watercress from the River Itchen

Shops and restaurants in the city

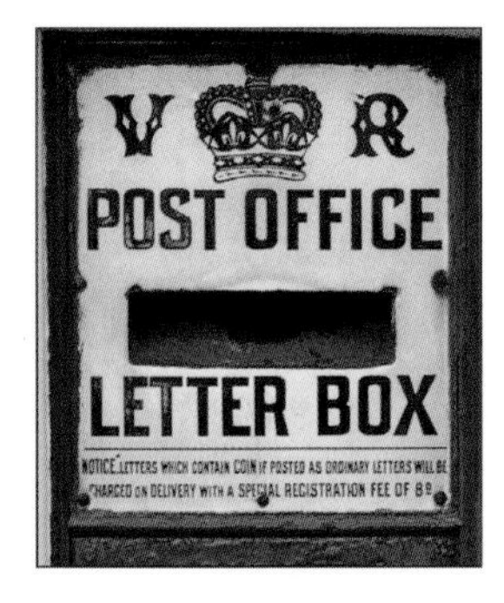

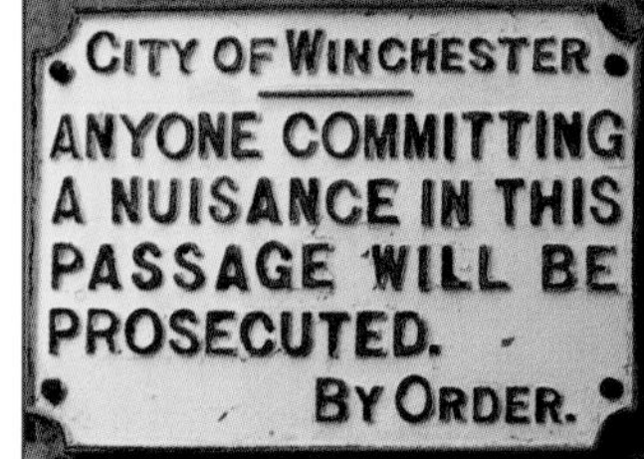

 Decorative and historic details in the city

The Guildhall towers over the mayoral residence and a sculpture in The Dean Garnier garden compliments the Cathedral's South Transept

52 Winchester High Street rooftops from the Westgate

Inside Winchester City Council Westgate Museum

54 Commemorative tableaux in The Gurkha Museum

WWII scout car at Peninsula Barracks

Peninsula Barracks

58 Bishop Morley College building in the Cathedral Outer Close

Patterned brickwork and autumn leaves

60 The Hospital of St Cross, founded in 1136 to provide sheltered accommodation and Alms

The Hospital stands about a mile out of the city in water meadows by the Itchen

62 Dawn at Twyford Down

Bridge over the River Itchen from Winchester College field

First published 2009 by Chris Andrews Publications Ltd

15 Curtis Yard North Hinksey Lane Oxford OX2 0LX Telephone: +44(0)1865 723404 **www.cap-ox.com**

Photos: Chris Andrews with additional images from Carole Andrews

ISBN 978-1-905385-99-7

Grateful thanks to VisitWinchester and to Winchester Cathedral for all help and permission to include images.

Front Cover: The Cathedral and City centre   Title page: The City at dawn   Back cover: Winchester College choristers
Endpapers: The City from the North and Medieval decorated floor tiles in the Cathedral

Chris Andrews

Chris Andrews work is known throughout England and the Channel Islands, and is seen in a variety of publications including calendars, posters, fine art prints and books.

This 'Little Souvenir' series attempts to show something of the unique charm of Winchester in an attractive and portable form and features the work of Chris and Carole Andrews
For information on all our publications see:

Chris Andrews Publications Ltd
www.cap-ox.co.uk